SPORTS GREATS

TOP 10 WIDE RECEIVERS IN FOOTBALL

SHERRI MABRY GORDON

Enslow Publishing
101 W. 23rd Street
Suite 240
New York, NY 10011
USA
enslow.com

Published in 2017 by Enslow Publishing, LLC.
101 W. 23rd Street, Suite 240, New York, NY 10011

Library of Congress Cataloging-in-Publication Data

TK from Ruby

Printed in China

To Our Readers: We have done our best to make sure all website addresses in this book were active and appropriate when we went to press. However, the author and the publisher have no control over and assume no liability for the material available on those websites or on any websites they may link to. Any comments or suggestions can be sent by email to customerservice@enslow.com.

Photo Credits: Cover, p. 1 Peter Read Miller/Sports Illustrated/Getty Images; pp. 4–5 © AP Images; p. 8 AP Photo/Pro Football Hall of Fame; p. 11 Allen Kee/Getty Images Sport/Getty Images; p. 13 Rogers Photo Archive/Getty Images Sport/Getty Images; p. 15 AP Photo/NFL Photos; p. 17 Charles Aqua Viva/ Getty Images Sport/Getty Images; p. 19 Peter Read Miller/Sports Illustrated/Getty Images; p. 21 Focus on Sport/Getty Images; p. 23 AP Photo/Vernon Biever; p. 25 Focus on Sport/Getty Images Sport/Getty Images; p. 27 John Biever/Sports Illustrated/Getty Images; p. 29 JEFF HAYNES/AFP/Getty Images; p. 31 Tom Dahlin/Sports Illustrated/Getty Images; p. 33 CRAIG LASSIG/AFP/Getty Images; p. 35 Tom Hauck/Allsport/Getty Images; p. 37 Al Bello/Getty Images Sport/Getty Images; p. 39 Harry How/Getty Images Sport/Getty Images; p. 41 Damian Strohmeyer/Sports Illustrated/Getty Images; p. 43 Gregory Shamus/Getty Images Sport/Getty Images; p. 44 Scott Cunningham/Getty Images Sport/Getty Images; design elements throughout book: maodoltee/Shutterstock.com (football field), RTimages/Shutterstock.com (grass), EsraKeskinSenay/Shutterstock.com (football stadium), Prixel Creative/Shutterstock.com (football play).

CONTENTS

INTRODUCTION

It's another diving catch for Pittsburgh Steelers' Lynn Swann during Super Bowl X in 1976 against the Dallas Cowboys. The Steelers won, and Swann was voted the game's MVP.

The nation's best wide receivers are some of the most gifted athletes around. They are the ones who can make the one-handed catches or bring down the long bombs and take them in for touchdowns. Wide receivers, or wideouts as they are sometimes called, have athleticism and skill that are unmatched by many athletes. As a result, they are often the go-to guys when a big play is needed.

To be a great wide receiver, a player usually has a unique combination of physical traits. At the top of the list are body control and agility. When an athlete is agile, he can change his body position, even while in the air, to make an important catch or play.

Just about any football player can run a passing route and turn around to catch a ball. The real challenge comes when the wideout is facing some of the best defenders around. He must be able to avoid the defense and still move his body in a way that allows him to catch the ball and make the play.

One of the best examples of this ability is Lynn Swann's amazing catch in Super Bowl X when the Pittsburgh Steelers faced the Dallas Cowboys. Late in the second quarter, Steelers quarterback Terry Bradshaw launched a 53-yard pass down the middle to Swann. For many players, this pass would have been uncatchable. But Swann dove for the ball, juggled it, and ultimately hauled down the pass all while cornerback Mark Washington was hanging onto him. Swann's big play is still one of the best examples of the superior athleticism that is required to be an outstanding wide receiver.

In addition to super athletic ability, the majority of successful wideouts are also strong, smart, focused, and fast. They also have sure, soft hands. Despite being hit by defenders, they are still able to catch the football. Cris Carter, who played the majority of his career for the Minnesota Vikings, had some of the softest hands of any wide receiver around. Football fans still enjoy watching the highlights from his career, many of which include one-handed catches.

On the flip side, many people view wide receivers as prima donnas with huge egos and demanding personalities who like to show off when they accomplish something big. Take for instance the time Terrell Owens danced on the star at the center of the Dallas Cowboys' field after scoring a touchdown. Football fans everywhere complained about that move.

Yet despite all this, there are not many football players who can do what wide receivers can do. They are the team's playmakers. They have a unique chemistry with the quarterback, mental toughness, and the ability to control their bodies even in extreme situations. As a result, they make some of the most remarkable plays on the football field—the kind we all like to watch over and over again. Check out some of the best that have ever played in the National Football League (NFL).

DON HUTSON

Nickname: Alabama Antelope

Team: Green Bay Packers (1935–1945)

Career Stats: 488 receptions; 7,991 yards; 99 touchdowns

Often referred to as the man who introduced football to the forward pass, Don Hutson dominated the wide receiver role in his time like no other. What's more, he held onto the honor as the top player in the NFL for the league's first fifty years. In fact, his record of 99 receiving touchdowns was not surpassed until forty years after he retired. And when he finally hung up his cleats in the mid-1940s, Hutson had logged nearly twice as many receptions as the next closest player.

Born in Pine Bluff, Arkansas, on January 31, 1913, Hutson played college football for the University of Alabama. After graduation, he played for the Green Bay Packers from 1935 to 1945. During that time, he played wide receiver but he was also a talented placekicker and defensive safety. But it was his skills as a receiver that helped set him apart. In fact, he was so good at what he did that he became the standard by which other wide receivers were judged. He also created many of the sport's passing routes that are still being used today.

When Hutson first took the field in 1935, no one knew what to expect. But they were soon to find out. The Packers were facing the Chicago Bears in their second game of the season, and Hutson was ready to show football fans what he could do. Standing on his own 17-yard line, Hutson took off as soon as the ball was snapped and raced past the Bears' secondary. Quarterback Arnie Herber passed him the ball, and Hutson exploded downfield for the only score of the

Don Hutson fights for a reception during an NFL game.

game. Most say it was that catch that birthed football's passing game.

According to football historian Jim Gigglioti, Green Bay purposefully did not play Hutson in the Packers' first game of 1935. They were saving him for their rivals, the Bears. And "on the first play against Chicago [Don Hutson] announced his arrival as the NFL's premier offensive threat."

Even though Hutson was not very big, his speed, precision, and soft hands kept opposing defenses on their toes. In fact, he became the first player in the NFL to be covered by two or more defenders.

By 1942, Hutson had his best season yet. He set NFL records by catching 74 passes for 1,211 yards and 17 touchdowns. He also kicked 33 extra points and one field goal for a total of 138 points. This feat remained the NFL single-season scoring record for nearly twenty years.

Don Hutson was selected as a member of the NFL's All-Pro team nine times and was named the league's Most Valuable Player in 1941 and 1942. When he retired, he had 488 pass receptions, a record that stood well into the late 1980s and shows just how far ahead of his peers Hutson was. Hutson was elected to the Pro Football Hall of Fame in 1963 as a member of the institution's inaugural class. He was also named to the NFL's 75th Anniversary All-Time Team in 1994.

Jerry Rice

Nickname: The GOAT

Teams: San Francisco 49ers (1985–2000); Oakland Raiders (2001–2004); Seattle Seahawks (2004)

Career Stats: 1,549 receptions; 22,895 yards; 197 touchdowns

Often referred to as the GOAT, or the "Greatest of All Time," Jerry Rice is one of the best wide receivers to ever play professional football. He was drafted in the first round by the San Francisco 49ers, but many were skeptical at first that Rice could have an impact in the NFL. After all, he did not start playing football until he was in high school. And his college career, although impressive, was not at one of the top-tier schools. Instead, he played football for Mississippi Valley State University.

Most NFL scouts thought Rice was too small and too slow to make an impact in professional football. Only Bill Walsh from San Francisco saw him differently, selecting him as the sixteenth pick in the first round of the draft.

Born October 13, 1962, in Starkville, Mississippi, Jerry was one of eight children and the son of a bricklayer.

During the hot summer months, Jerry and his brothers worked alongside their father. The work was grueling, but Rice later said it taught him the meaning of hard work, an attribute that was clearly displayed throughout his impressive career.

Rice's first season in the NFL did not go as smoothly as most expected, though. Although he earned Rookie of the Year honors, caught 49 balls for 927 yards, and scored 3 touchdowns, his season was marred by a series of dropped balls, which were uncharacteristic

After a rocky first year with the 49ers, Jerry Rice went on to play for twenty seasons and became one of the best wide receivers football has ever seen.

for him. But just a year later he logged his first of eleven consecutive 1,000-yard seasons with an impressive 1,570 yards in 1986. This feat earned him his first trip to the Pro Bowl and his first selection as an All-Pro.

Rice seemed to save his most exciting performances for when the team really needed a big play. For instance, in 1988 as the 49ers began their march toward the Super Bowl that year, a young Rice showed the nation that he was a scoring threat. In just week two of that season, the 49ers were down 17–13 in the closing minutes of the game. Quarterback Joe Montana sent a deep pass down the right sideline to Rice. Not only did Rice catch the ball, but he also eluded two defenders who collided on the field while trying to catch him. Rice skillfully slipped past them and hauled in a 78-yard touchdown.

In the 1987 season, the Cincinnati Bengals were leading the 49ers 26–20 with just seconds to play. For some reason, the Bengals left Rice alone in the corner of the end zone. Joe Montana spotted his star receiver and gunned the ball right to him. Rice jumped up to catch the pass and there was not a defender in sight. That day, football coaches and players alike discovered that "you never, ever single-cover Jerry Rice in any situation," said Jon Gruden, former NFL football coach.

From the beginning, it was clear that Rice's work ethic, explosiveness at the snap, and perfectionist personality were going to take him straight to the top. Even today, Jerry Rice is so far ahead of everyone in receptions (1,549), yards (22,895), and touchdown catches (197) that his records will probably never be surpassed. Rice once had thirteen consecutive games with a touchdown and 274 consecutive games with a catch. Before his career was over, Rice made twelve more trips to the Pro Bowl and made the All-Pro team eleven more times. Not only was Rice a remarkable wide receiver, but he also is arguably one of the world's premier athletes. Much of this success is due to the fact that he played professional football for more than twenty seasons.

The athletic Jerry Rice pulls in a pass for a touchdown.

LANCE ALWORTH

NICKNAME: BAMBI

TEAMS: SAN DIEGO CHARGERS (1962–1970); DALLAS COWBOYS (1971–1972)

CAREER STATS: 542 RECEPTIONS; 10,266 YARDS; 85 TOUCHDOWNS

When the American Football League (AFL) came onto the scene in the 1960s, the NFL suddenly had some competition for securing the best football players. What resulted was an intense bidding war between the two leagues to secure the top talent from the draft. One of the first players to experience the bidding war was wide receiver Lance Alworth. The AFL operated from 1960 to 1969 before merging with the NFL, and Alworth was one of the premier stars of the league.

Born on August 3, 1940, in Houston, Texas, Lance was the son of an oilfield construction executive and a teacher. During high school, Lance excelled in a number of sports. In fact, he won fifteen letters in four sports, including baseball, basketball, football, and track. His natural athletic ability even caught the eye of both the New York Yankees and the Pittsburgh Pirates. Both professional baseball teams offered him contracts to

Lance Alworth played for nine seasons with the San Diego Chargers. This shot was taken at training camp in 1969.

play right out of high school. Instead, Lance followed his father's advice and played college football while also earning a degree.

When Alworth graduated from the University of Arkansas in 1962, teams in both the AFL and the NFL wanted him. In fact, he was picked eighth overall in the NFL draft by the San Francisco 49ers and was selected ninth overall in the AFL draft by the Oakland Raiders. But not long after the draft, the Raiders traded Alworth to the San Diego Chargers in exchange for other players.

Still, it was up to Alworth to decide where he would play. Ultimately, he signed with the Chargers. While at San Diego, Alworth earned the nickname "Bambi" because he had a baby face and could run like a deer. Even though he tried to get rid of the nickname throughout the years, such as by changing his hairstyle, it stuck with him for his entire career.

Overall, Alworth says he can count only six dropped passes during his twenty-one-year career. This is a remarkable accomplishment considering the fact that defensive backs could bump receivers all the way down the field at that time. Today they cannot do that.

But his consistency in catching passes was something that took work. In fact, there is one game in particular that Alworth says changed his entire mindset. During a game against the Chiefs, defensive back Fred "the Hammer" Williams was getting under his skin with his constant bumping and trash talking. And as a result, Alworth dropped three balls in that game.

"I wanted to get away [from him] so quick that I'd leave the ball there," Alworth recalled in an interview with the *New York Daily News*. "[When] I looked at the film, I was so ticked off. I was taking off right before [the ball] got there."

After that, Alworth says he figured out a little routine that he made himself do every day. "It was a simple thing: watch it, catch it and tuck it," he recalls. "I'd watch it come into my hands. I would watch my hands catch it. I would watch my hands put it away. I didn't take my eyes off it the whole time."

With this leaping catch in December 1969, Lance Alworth broke Don Hutson's record for the number of consecutive games with a catch, upping it to 96.

By the 1965 and 1966 seasons, this little routine proved especially successful. Alworth put together the best back-to-back campaigns a receiver has ever had according to the NFL. In those two seasons, he averaged more than 110 yards a game. He also averaged one touchdown per game with more than 20 yards per catch. These accomplishments allowed him to become the first true AFL player elected to the Pro Football Hall of Fame.

STEVE LARGENT

Team: Seattle Seahawks (1976–1989)

Career Stats: 819 receptions; 13,089 yards; 100 touchdowns

When Steve Largent was drafted as the 117th pick in 1976, it was more of an afterthought than anything else. And yet Largent went on to lead the NFL in career receptions, yards, and touchdown catches at the time of his retirement.

Born September 28, 1954, in Tulsa, Oklahoma, Steve was an impressive high school football player. But when college scouts did not heavily recruit him, he enrolled at the lesser-known University of Tulsa in his hometown. After he graduated in 1976, he had completed one of the best football careers in Tulsa football history.

The Houston Oilers drafted Largent in the fourth round of the draft. But he never appeared in their uniform. Instead, the Oilers traded him to the Seattle Seahawks, where he spent his entire career.

By the end of the 1976 season, the Oilers realized they had made a terrible mistake in letting Largent go.

At just under 6 feet tall (183 centimeters), Steve was not built like the typical professional wideout of the 1980s. But he more than made up for his small frame with his intelligence and his sheer determination to succeed in a league where most people thought he did not stand a chance.

He had a willingness to work the middle. He was also able to break tackles after catching the ball and add extra yards to his plays. This fact was part of the reason he was able to finish his career averaging 16 yards per catch.

Steve Largent stretches before a 1986 game against the Redskins.

What's more, Largent came up with big plays when his team needed it. For instance, in the 1983 division play-offs in Miami, Largent helped the Seahawks upset the favored Miami Dolphins. Although he was held scoreless for the first fifty-seven minutes of the game, he produced a 40-yard touchdown on the final drive of the game that helped the Seahawks secure the win.

"Few receivers can read routes and coverages and make adjustments like he can," former teammate and defensive back Dave Brown told *People* magazine.

Over the course of his fourteen seasons, Largent raised the bar for wide receivers, catching 70 or more passes six times. He also set a record by catching at least one pass in 177 straight games and led the NFL in receiving twice, once in 1979 and once in 1985.

Overall, the former Seattle Seahawk logged eight 1,000-yard seasons, despite playing through two strikes. Keep in mind this occurred in the late 1970s and 1980s, when football teams were just starting to incorporate passing into the game. So this was a huge accomplishment at the time. By the time he retired, Largent held every major receiving record and was the first player to catch 100 touchdown passes.

Largent was named to the Pro Bowl seven times during his career and was inducted into the Pro Football Hall of Fame in 1995.

JAMES LOFTON

TEAMS: GREEN BAY PACKERS (1978–1986);
LOS ANGELES RAIDERS (1987–1988);
BUFFALO BILLS (1989–1992);
PHILADELPHIA EAGLES (1993);
LOS ANGELES RAMS (1993)

CAREER STATS: 764 RECEPTIONS; 14,004 YARDS; 75 TOUCHDOWNS

James Lofton started out as a college track-and-field star at Stanford before becoming one of football's greatest wide receivers. But it was not until his senior year at the university that he finally made his mark in football. After that he logged an impressive sixteen-year career in the NFL that spanned almost three decades of football. What's more, it was Lofton's record of 14,004 yards that Jerry Rice had to break in order to jump to the top.

Born at Fort Ord, a military base in California, on July 5, 1956, James grew up with a single dad. In the beginning, James's football career took a backseat to track and field. For instance, he would miss spring football camp because of track competitions.

Consequently, during his first three years at Stanford, he was never a top-tier player. Even by the time he finished college, Lofton was known more for his achievements on the track than he was for his efforts on the football field. Not only was he a respected sprinter at Stanford, including placing fifth in a sprint event at the 1976 US Olympic trials, but he also had won the NCAA long jump title.

James Lofton averaged 17.7 yards per catch during his rookie year. He was selected for the Pro Bowl that year, the first of eight Pro Bowl selections during his career.

Yet, his football accomplishments still caught the eye of pro scouts. Lofton was selected sixth in the 1978 NFL draft. He was a first round pick for the Green Bay Packers. This selection also meant that he would experience playing in cold weather for the first time in his life. But it didn't take him long to adjust to the new climate.

In his rookie year, Lofton caught 46 passes for 818 yards and 6 touchdowns. In his third season with Green Bay, Lofton surpassed the 1,000-yard mark for the first time with 1,221 yards and caught a career-high 71 receptions. And he was making memorable plays while he was at it.

One notable highlight includes the 1981 NFC first-round play-off game against the St. Louis Cardinals. Lofton caught a 20-yard touchdown pass to lead the Packers to a 41–16 win. Then one game later, he showed his skills again when he hauled in a 6-yard touchdown reception and a 71-yard touchdown return on a blocked kick. Despite the fact that he scored almost half of the Packers' points, they still lost 37–26 to the Dallas Cowboys. But his highlight reel from the game is still impressive.

By 1986, when his numbers started to fall below 1,000 yards, he was traded to the Los Angeles Raiders. By the end of the 1988 season, the Raiders cut him as well. At this point, it seemed like his career was over, but Lofton was picked up by the Buffalo Bills. The move seemed to jump-start his career. In fact, he played for the Bills in three Super Bowls.

His most memorable plays while he was there included the first touchdown of the AFC championship against the Raiders and a 61-yard reception against the Giants in Super Bowl XXV. Meanwhile, his best game with the Bills was against the Bengals in 1991. He had eight catches for 220 yards and two touchdowns in that game.

Lofton played in three Super Bowls with the Buffalo Bills. Here, he catches a pass during Super Bowl XXVI against the Redskins.

That same year, at the age of thirty-five, Lofton became the oldest player in NFL history to top 1,000 yards in pass reception. After the Bills, he later played briefly for the Los Angeles Rams and the Philadelphia Eagles before retiring. He was inducted into the Pro Football Hall of Fame in 2003.

MICHAEL IRVIN

NICKNAME: THE PLAYMAKER

TEAM NAME: DALLAS COWBOYS (1988–1999)

CAREER STATS: 750 RECEPTIONS; 11,904 YARDS; 65 TOUCHDOWNS

Even though Michael Irvin was referred to as "the Playmaker," some would argue that his stats do not meet the criteria for a top-ten list of wide receivers. But keep in mind, his career was cut short when he suffered a severe neck injury and doctors advised him to stop playing. Had he been allowed to continue, he likely would have racked up even higher numbers. Combine this with the fact that Irvin was instrumental in multiple championships and anyone can see why he makes the cut.

Born on March 5, 1966, in Ft. Lauderdale, Florida, Michael was the fifteenth of seventeen children. His family was very poor, and his house had only two bedrooms. Eventually, Michael's father converted the porch and garage into extra living space, but Michael never had his own bed until he went to college.

Irvin decided to play college football close to home after his father died suddenly. As a result, he played for the University of Miami under head coach Jimmy

Johnson. During his time there, Irvin helped lead the team to a national championship.

In 1988, Irvin was the eleventh pick in the draft and headed to the Dallas Cowboys. He used his $1.8-million contract to buy his mom a four-bedroom house with a swimming pool. He also supplied her with the first credit card she had ever owned. Once in Dallas, his career took off. He quickly became the team's starting wide receiver.

On December 11, Irvin showed what he could do against the rival Redskins. During that game, he caught

During Super Bowl XXVII, Irvin was not shy about celebrating his touchdown.

six passes and scored three touchdowns as the Cowboys secured a victory. That day was significant for another reason. It was head coach Tom Landry's last game in Dallas. The new owner fired coach Landry and hired Jimmy Johnson, Irvin's former college coach.

But Irvin didn't get to play much during Johnson's first season there. He tore an anterior cruciate ligament in his left knee in the sixth game of the season. As a result, he sat out the remainder of the season.

By 1991, Irvin had recovered and showed football fans everywhere that he had what it took to make a mark as a wideout in the NFL. During that season he became the leading receiver in the nation and earned his first invitation to the Pro Bowl. All in all, Irvin made five consecutive Pro Bowl appearances.

The next two seasons, Irvin—along with quarterback Troy Aikman and running back Emmitt Smith—won back-to-back Super Bowls for the Cowboys. In the 1994 Super Bowl, Irvin thrilled Cowboy fans across the nation by making two touchdowns on receptions in the span of just fifteen seconds, leading the Cowboys to a 52–17 trouncing of the Buffalo Bills.

In 1999, Irvin's career was cut short when he suffered a serious neck injury and had to give up the game he loved. Many wonder what he could have done in the NFL had he not been injured. Irvin was inducted into the Pro Football Hall of Fame eight years later.

Michael Irvin (*left*) and quarterback Troy Aikman (*right*) celebrate Emmitt Smith's touchdown during a 1996 NFC championship game. The three stars later led the Cowboys to a victory against the Pittsburgh Steelers in Super Bowl XXX.

RANDY MOSS

NICKNAME: THE FREAK

TEAMS: MINNESOTA VIKINGS (1998–2004, 2010); OAKLAND RAIDERS (2005–2006); NEW ENGLAND PATRIOTS (2007–2010); TENNESSEE TITANS (2010); SAN FRANCISCO 49ERS (2011)

CAREER STATS: 982 RECEPTIONS; 15,292 YARDS; 156 TOUCHDOWNS

Randy "the Freak" Moss was one of the greatest athletes in the NFL. At 6 feet, 4 inches (193 cm) and with a 40-yard dash time of 4.25, Moss's physical gifts allowed him leap past defenders for deep passes, jump over fallen bodies, and outrace anyone into the end zone.

In fact, if it were not for his tendency to get into trouble, he probably would have had a much smoother career. Instead, his antics saw him lose out on opportunities to play college football at both Notre Dame and Florida State; ultimately, he attended Marshal University after both colleges dropped their scholarship offers.

The Vikings went 15–1 and scored the most points in the history of the NFL during Randy Moss's rookie year.

A native of Rand, West Virginia, Randy was born February 13, 1977. He first showed potential as a star wideout in high school. He also played defensive back and was a special teams all-star. During the off-season he played basketball and baseball and ran track. While in high school, Randy led his team to two state championships. He was also named West Virginia Football Player of the Year in 1994.

In 1998, Moss was drafted to the NFL as the twenty-first pick by the Minnesota Vikings, and he took the league by storm. In that year, he tallied 1,313 yards on 69 catches for 17 touchdowns, breaking the rookie record.

Then in 1999, Moss caught his first one-handed pass in the NFL. During a 26–16 win over Tennessee, Moss effortlessly jumped over cornerback Denard Walker on a two-point conversion. Not long after that, defensive coordinators began to fear him more than any other player in the NFL. In fact, Moss was so dominant that a new term for a jump ball that is caught was coined: "getting Moss'd."

In 2005, the Vikings traded Moss to the Oakland Raiders. But his two years in Oakland were unproductive, and by 2007 he was traded again to the New England Patriots. While there, Moss quickly turned his career around. Teamed with quarterback Tom Brady, Moss and the Patriots posted the first 16–0

Randy Moss jumps to catch a Randall Cunningham pass against the Green Bay Packers.

regular season record in the NFL. They also broke the Vikings' single-season scoring mark. Moss also broke Jerry Rice's twenty-year-old NFL record by catching 23 touchdown passes.

In 2009, Moss caught his 141st career touchdown pass. This feat was the second-highest total in NFL history behind Jerry Rice. Despite his troubles off the football field, Moss had an amazing ability to read coverage and get open. In fact, Bill Belichick, the coach of the Patriots, described Moss as one of the most intelligent receivers he has ever coached.

TERRELL OWENS

NICKNAME: T.O.

TEAMS: SAN FRANCISCO 49ERS (1996–2003); PHILADELPHIA EAGLES (2004–2005); DALLAS COWBOYS (2006–2008); BUFFALO BILLS (2009); CINCINNATI BENGALS (2010)

CAREER STATS: 1,078 RECEPTIONS; 15,934 YARDS; 153 TOUCHDOWNS

Terrell Owens, or T.O. as many called him, was a force to be reckoned with. But life was not always easy for him. Born December 7, 1973, in Alexander City, Alabama, T.O. had a hard life. Living with a single mother and an abusive and alcoholic grandmother, he immersed himself in sports to escape. Basketball, baseball, and swimming were his favorites, but he also liked football and idolized San Francisco star Jerry Rice.

During high school, T.O. lettered four times in football and track. He also earned three letters in basketball and one in baseball. Surprisingly, Terrell did not start on the football team until his senior year. He even thought about quitting. But his coaches talked him out of it.

After high school, the University of Tennessee offered him the opportunity to compete in multiple sports at the collegiate level. While in college, Owens was a forward on the basketball team for three years. He also anchored the school's 4 x 100 relay team. However, it was his efforts on the football field that set him apart. Wearing number 80 in honor of his hero, Jerry Rice, Owens showed professional scouts that he could catch footballs and score touchdowns.

Terrell Owens was delighted to be drafted by the San Francisco 49ers, where he starred as a wide receiver for seven years. He and QB Steve Young made quite a team.

When it came time for the draft, the San Francisco 49ers expressed some interest in T.O. and the thought of playing with his hero and catching passes from Steve Young was almost too much for Owens to hope for. But it happened. The 49ers picked him in the third round as the eighty-ninth pick overall, and he could barely contain his excitement.

During his first season in San Francisco, T.O. contributed a great deal on special teams. He also caught 35 passes for 520 yards and 4 touchdowns. Then when Jerry Rice was out with a torn ACL, Owens was able to show the league what he could do. He became one of quarterback Steve Young's top targets.

By 1999, Owens was sidelined with an injury but made a comeback the next year. In fact, 2000 was one of the best years of his career. He logged 1,451 yards receiving and scored 13 touchdowns in just 14 games. In 2004, Owens was traded to the Philadelphia Eagles. Later, he played for the Dallas Cowboys, the Buffalo Bills, and the Cincinnati Bengals.

One of the greatest moments in Owens's football career occurred during Super Bowl XXXIX. It was his first season with the Philadelphia Eagles. But early on it looked like he would not be able to participate in the Super Bowl. Owens had sprained a ligament in his ankle and had to have a screw implanted. Then, he fractured his fibula. Most felt the season was over for him. Even though he was diligent and worked hard with rehab, the doctors refused to clear him to play in the Super Bowl. But Owens had other plans. He was determined he would play if the Eagles made it that far. To do so, he had to sign waivers just to be able to take the field.

Many considered this game between the Philadelphia Eagles and the New England Patriots one of the most

Even though the Eagles lost Super Bowl XXXIX by a score of 24–21, Owens did not disappoint his fans. He caught nine passes for 122 yards, shocking the Patriots with his abilities.

courageous performances in Super Bowl history. Even Owens was excited about his performance. "I'm on half a leg and they can't stop me," he later said.

After the Eagles, Owens played for the Bills. While there, he racked up 1,000 career receptions, becoming only the sixth NFL player to reach that mark. Then, while playing with the Bengals in 2010, he suffered a torn ACL during the off-season. This injury ended his fifteen-year career.

MARVIN HARRISON

TEAM: INDIANAPOLIS COLTS (1996–2008)

CAREER STATS: 1,102 RECEPTIONS; 14,580 YARDS; 128 TOUCHDOWNS

Marvin Harrison is widely considered one of the greatest and most productive wide receivers in NFL history. Like the Jerry Rice and Joe Montana combo, Harrison had the benefit of catching balls from future Hall of Fame quarterback Peyton Manning.

Born August 25, 1972, in Philadelphia, Pennsylvania, Harrison first turned heads as a receiver at Syracuse University. During his senior year in 1995, he nabbed 56 passes and racked up 1,131 yards and 8 touchdowns in 11 games. Going into the 1996 draft, Harrison was one of the top-ranked receivers on the board. He was the nineteenth overall pick and headed to the Indianapolis Colts. Harrison would play his entire career in Indianapolis.

During his time with the Colts, Harrison and Manning were the most productive receiver and quarterback pairing in NFL history. What's more, Harrison's statistics rival those of Jerry Rice. For instance, his 1,102 career receptions are the third most in league history behind only Rice (1,549) and tight end Tony Gonzalez (1,325).

But you would never hear much about this success from him. One thing that set Harrison apart from other wideouts was his quiet demeanor. In fact, most wide receivers like to talk about their accomplishments. But Harrison let his plays speak for themselves. He would do his job on the field and then head to the locker room.

Marvin Harrison spent his entire NFL career starring with the Indianapolis Colts.

What's more, ask just about any defender from that time period who was the toughest wide receiver to cover and they would likely say Marvin Harrison. In fact, Charles Tillman, a longtime Bears cornerback says Harrison was one of the toughest receivers he ever played against. "I could never touch him, never jam him," Tillman told *Sports Illustrated*. "He was so quick, like a little rabbit. I missed every time."

Additionally, Harrison's plays were fun to watch. In fact, many people have said Harrison was "a highlight reel waiting to happen." Everything he did on the field showed his superior athletic ability and his uncanny ability to find the end zone.

While there are so many great moments in Harrison's career, the one that stands out to most people is his one-handed catch in 2003 against the Tennessee Titans. Not only did he catch the ball with one hand, but he also had the body control and field awareness to get both feet on the ground before he landed out of bounds.

After he injured his leg in 2007, Harrison missed an NFL game for the first time since 1998. That year, he only played in five games the entire season, by far the lowest in his career.

In 2008, Harrison returned and played in fifteen games. But his time in Indianapolis was coming to a close. He was released from the Colts following the 2008 season. Harrison expected that they would sign

Harrison's one-handed grab against Tennessee in 2003 is a play that has been watched over and over again.

him back at a later date but that never happened. As a result, he sat out the entire season in 2009. Instead of going the same route as Jerry Rice and signing with another team for less money and playing time, Harrison hung up his cleats and retired from the NFL. In 2016, he was selected into the Pro Football Hall of Fame.

CALVIN JOHNSON

NICKNAME: MEGATRON

TEAM: DETROIT LIONS (2007–2015)

CAREER STATS: 731 RECEPTIONS; 11,619 YARDS; 83 TOUCHDOWNS

Although Calvin Johnson's career was short, he still makes the list because of what he accomplished in those few short years. For instance, from 2011 to 2013, Johnson, or "Megatron" as he was sometimes called, was considered the best wide receiver in pro football at the time. During that time, he produced three of the best seasons a wideout could hope to have, averaging more than 110 yards per game.

In just nine short seasons, Johnson compiled some impressive stats, and many felt he would surpass Jerry Rice's records had he continued playing.

"He'll be a first-ballot [Hall of Fame] guy," Ronnie Lott, one of Johnson's former teammates said. "In those nine seasons he's allowed all of us to know that he can be just as good as Jerry Rice. And that's key."

Johnson was born on September 29, 1985, in Newnan, Georgia. He was the second of Arica and Calvin Sr.'s four kids. As one of the tallest boys in his class, Johnson stood 6 feet (183 cm) at age twelve and reached a height of 6 feet, 3 inches (190 cm) as a sophomore in high school. That year, he also became a starting wide receiver.

By the end of high school, some scouting services had Johnson ranked among the top twenty players in the nation and the number one player in the state. But he surprised everyone when he accepted a scholarship from Georgia Tech. Although the school's coach had run offenses in the NFL before, it was the school's engineering program that was the deciding factor.

Calvin Johnson pulls in a touchdown pass against the Philadelphia Eagles in 2015.

By 2007, Johnson declared himself ready for NFL draft, and he was unquestionably the best player coming out of college. He became the third pick in the first round of the draft when the Detroit Lions nabbed him. Once Lions' teammate Roy Williams saw the gigantic rookie, he nicknamed him Megatron after the Transformers robot. And the nickname stuck.

Johnson's time with the Lions was impressive. In almost every game he played, he made an unbelievable catch. By 2011, he set career highs with 16 touchdowns and an NFL-best 1,681 yards, helping the Lions achieve a 10–6 record and their first play-off appearance since 1999.

Calvin Johnson retired after the 2015 season, but not before earning six Pro Bowl invitations.

One of Johnson's most impressive performances that year came during the fourth game of the season. He helped rally the Lions from a 24-point deficit with two touchdowns in the fourth quarter, one of which was under triple coverage in the end zone. With Johnson's help, the Lions went on to beat the Cowboys 34–30.

Johnson had become a valuable asset, and the Detroit Lions wanted to keep him around. Before the 2012 NFL season rolled around, they gave him a seven-year, $132-million contract extension. This deal not only made him the highest-paid receiver in the NFL but also the highest-paid player at any position in the NFL.

Before his retirement, Johnson was on par with Jerry Rice's production. For instance, he broke Rice's single-season receiving mark in 2012. He also averaged 86.1 yards per game, which beat Rice's 75.6 average. But he did not come close to Rice's longevity when his length in the NFL was cut short.

Johnson hung up his cleats in 2016 after battling through an array of injuries. He had a painful knee injury in 2013 that required weekly drains. In 2014, he suffered a high ankle sprain that cost him three games and limited him in two others. Meanwhile, another ankle injury in 2015 cost him valuable practice time.

Yet despite his short stint in the NFL and his multiple injuries, Johnson logged some impressive stats. He also holds nearly every significant Detroit Lions record.

GLOSSARY

AFL The American Football League, which operated from 1960 to 1969. The AFL was created by a number of owners who had been refused NFL expansion franchises.

agility The ability to change the body's position, even in midair.

coverage A defensive scheme in football used to protect against the pass.

linebacker A member of the defensive team that provides extra run protection or extra pass protection on the defensive play.

passing route A path or pattern that a receiver runs to get open for a forward pass.

prima donna A player who thinks he is better than everyone else and does not work well as part of a group.

rookie A first-year player in a professional sport; they are considered rookies because they are inexperienced at that level of play.

safety A member of the defensive team that is often considered the last line of defense; they usually cover the middle and sidelines and are often considered the hardest hitters in football.

screen A play designed to deceive the defense into believing the quarterback will drop back and throw downfield; instead he either hands the ball off or throws a short pass.

snap The motion that begins the play in football; it typically occurs when the center passes the ball back to the quarterback.

soft hands A trait of a player who is able to catch the football without bobbling it or using his chest or body.

tight end A position in football often considered a hybrid between a wide receiver and an offensive lineman.

wideout Another name for a wide receiver.

wide receiver An offensive position in football and the key player in most passing plays; wide receivers are usually the fastest and most agile players in the game.